CHRYSALIS

Branden Polk
Chrysalis

Published by BooxAI
ISBN: 978-965-578-572-2

CHRYSALIS

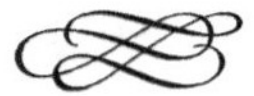

BRANDEN POLK

INTRODUCTION

Denaus Plexipus. Otherwise known as Monarch Butterflies. The bright colors, oranges, and blacks mingled together, with their unusually large wingspan – as butterflies go – offered a touch of hope during a very uncertain, unstable, and unsustainable season. Why? Well, it's because they weren't always butterflies. It's because they were something else and then transformed into a greater and more authentic expression of the thing it was before. I still feel like a caterpillar; don't get me wrong. But I am also experiencing a process that I must go through in order to become a beautiful, courageous butterfly.

What is that process? For the caterpillar, the cocoon, or the chrysalis, is where the temperature is turned up. I know that when I was in grade school, we tended to skip right to the part in the National Geographic documentary that captures the new creature's miraculous emergence. No one ever stopped to ask the most obvious questions about what the actual fuck is going on in that oven! I'm convinced now that they didn't tell us on purpose because it's at least Rated R and therefore not suitable for children. This poor, unsuspecting caterpillar is enclosed in a

tiny space where it is basically melted, '*deconstituted*' and liqui-
fied. Doesn't sound so great to me.

My inaugural book of poems, entitled *Chrysalis*, is written in the
first person. It is an exploration of discomfort and uncertainty.
Of beauty, wonder, and love. Of joy and loss. The ups and
downs that one must go through in order to gain the strength to
emerge as something different, authentic, weird, vulnerable, and
real. REAL. The hope is real, but so is the pain. The sorrow is
real, but so is the love. I am sharing with you some of my most
treasured and complex memories, my clumsy journey through
identity discovery.

It's my belief that we are all still learning, as we squirm around
in this entangled and encaged life, that breaking through to the
outer layers is not an exercise of weakness. It is rather a mercy
or a grace that somehow constrains us, compelling us to push
free, to unfold the left wing and the right wing, spreading them
out as far as possible, leaping into the next beautiful,
extraordinary, and dangerous chapter.

FORBIDDEN LOVE POEM

Broken heart tonight,
That wants to sing songs.
With memory so close,
Yet twinges of pain twisting and digging,
As dissonant tones unheard
Scream, mobilizing louder feelings.

The aforementioned grieving heart,
Was once in love forbidden,
Allured by ONE soul.
Intoxicating, but pure —
So pure is the addiction.
Unrestrained, perpetual affliction.

It is a fire that cannot be wavered.
Unquenchable, unsatisfied flame,
Scarring very deeply — in a place
Seen only by God.

Almost perceived by another – human.

ALL THAT WE'VE BEEN GOING THROUGH

All that we've been going through,
It's not hard to blame it on you.
Yes, you had us sitting in only negativity,
For yourself – you took all that you needed — from me.

Think this is funny? Are you amused at my reaction?
Criticized and abused.
The truth is —
That you are so down on you,
Jealousy-ravaged like a toxic goo.

Time still rages forward.
We need to say, 'Thank you'.
We want to say 'Thank you' —
For letting *us* go.
It's not worth more time spent.

We need to say 'Thank you'.
We want to say 'Thank you' —

For showing *us* the truth.
— that you were no good, always.

HATRED

I'm trying really hard,
Not to hate you,
For not loving me.

You see —
That person that you're with right now,
Will never love you,
Oh no, not the way that I love you.

And yet,
You keep going back,
Like something is going to change.

I suppose I am guilty of the same —
The way —
I keep hoping that you'll see me,
That you'll hug me,
That you will go away with me.
In the end, it is a fantasy.

This causes me to freak out in a way --
'single white female-ish' or *'godfather-ish'*,
I want to lash out and separate;
Disintegrate myself from you because it hurts
Just too much for sanity to remain,
To be around, to not be enough.

The pain will go on and on,
With no end in time or in rhyme.
The hope of our closeness is dying
It will not stop or hide.
See it on my face
    — rejection
    — fear
    — unmet longings
That I dare to admit, are only for you.

God has hated me,
She doomed me to breathe without love's devotion.
Half-hearted and unsure.
I want more for my life, yet unwilling to unyield.

One day, a good sense shall return.
My head and heart will bloom from the turmoil, the downpour.
At the asinine notion of hope —
A hope that makes one ignorant and naive.
A hope that leaves one alone with true promise.
My hope is painful, unflawed.

Hope — please stay close,
and strengthen my heart.
Let go of hardness, lengthen love.

Hope — kept from the hell of hatred and
Preserved from anger and bitterness within.

ASKING YOU FOR 'THINGS'

I feel like,
I ask you,
I wait to see if you will do those *'things.'*
I'm still waiting…

The length of time between when I asked you,
Then, not seeing.
This has led me to a place of doubt —

This is not a doubt in your existence,
Or a questioning of your power.
These ever-vexing questions arise even so.

Do you love me?
Do you see my pain?
My anguish?

I know you have the power to change *'things.'*
So, I wonder why
You do not help.

This *why* is important to me.

Maybe you don't come close
Because I'm not clean.
Maybe because I've made mistakes.
Maybe this is punitive.

I am the lack of ____

Am I not good enough for you?
Why do you bring me to this place of connection,
Only to leave me by myself?

Why does he need to be here?
Why do you open up to him instead of me?

Are you curious about what's in my mind,
Or about what is happening in my body?
Who will touch me first?
God, where is your blessing?

To the left behind,
To those left alone,
Aspire evermore,
To understand,
Those *'things'*.

DISRESPECTED

Mishandled.
Misunderstood.
Left out.
Do I deserve to feel unloved because of the choices I made?

But not you.
Your errors were egregious.
I stood by you. I called you friend.

You stood there and told me that it wasn't 'ok' for me to talk.
You made me feel like I wasn't allowed to speak.

What's really not 'ok' is your tone, your meanness.
I am not an ignorant person,
Yet you make me feel as though I can't have an opinion
On the *issues of the day*.
I know what's out there.
I've lived.
Just like you.

I should never have had a friend like you —
Someone who treats me the way you do.

You take all the legitimate choices that I've made
and twisted them so that everyone thinks I'm the crazy one.

You know what, though?

I am allowed to be different.
I am allowed to think differently,
To believe something other than what you think I should.

Until you, I was able to make friends of different backgrounds,
With different points of view.
So, who is the problem here really?
Is it me?
Or is it you?

Instead, you'd rather minimize me in order to feel better about
yourself.

So many times you made me feel small.
You were never for me.
Never at all.
You left me abandoned and alone.
You weren't a real friend.
You were never for me.
Never at all.

I gave you the benefit of the doubt,
That you would love me no matter what.
Now I'm grieving, this thing that can never be with us.

How dare you treat me this way?
How dare you hurt me when I stood up for you?
No matter how hard I tried, no matter what I put on the floor —
(I left it all on the floor).

I left it all on the floor,
But you left and never said you were sorry.
You never said you cared.
You left, without warning,
Turning everyone against me.

You poisoned the well, and now you have to live with it.
—But you don't live with it.
—You don't consider it.
—You just move on from it, all destruction in your wake.

All this pain in your wake.
All the promises you destroyed.
You have taken away innocence.
My zeal.
My heart.
Ruined.

It has changed forever because of what you have done.

Oh, How I long to be restored!
How I long for justification!
How I long for vindication!
Where is there someone who will validate my soul?
Where is justice while my accusers prosper?
Where is God?

I WAS IN LOVE, ONCE.

I met you,
in class in the year 2000.
I met you,
But I didn't think twice about you.

I met you,
In the shadow of others who had my initial attention.
They were louder and
Seemingly more fun than you.

I met you,
With short hair, ripped jeans
And a sarcasm that could cut to the center of diamonds.
You cut deeply,
With your brown eyes --
But I did not see you.

After I met you,
I heard you say to me,
"Can we hang out sometime?"

Naively, I said *'yes'* without knowing what you really meant.
I mean, being 'just friends' –
Was fine with me.
(I can always use more friends, right?)
Well, you had more on your mind.
I wasn't giving you the time.

Six months went by.
We spent every Saturday
Making pancakes with
Chocolate chips and blueberries.

"Don't forget the whipped cream!"

(I always forgot the whipped cream.)

"Can I ask you something?"

Sure. Sure you can.
You can ask me anything.

"Don't you know that you're my boyfriend?"

Umm no.
I did not know that.
Why would you even say that?

"Every Saturday, we make pancakes, and we talk,
About life.
We laugh,
About life and
We dream."

Hmm, I suppose we do spend a lot of time together,
But that doesn't mean that ...

"Tell me that you don't feel it."

Beat.
Beat.

Watering of the eyes.
I cannot lie.
I cannot say it.
I'm about to be caught in a lie.
But the look on my face is not denying
– that I feel it too.

No words.
I'm about to say something, but then ...

"I love you.
I've loved you for a long time."

Shocked.
Stunned.
No air. Can't breathe.
(I'm going to make the wrong choice. I'm going to say the
wrong thing.)

I hate you for this.
This --
Is too hard.
This --
Is too risky.

I love you too.
From the first time that I saw you.
It's true.
Oh, it's true.
At first sight, I fell. Not capable of imagining my life without
you.

Now I've done it!
Joy is here. Joy escapes me because
Now I'm afraid I'll lose you.

But …
One tear shed tells it all.
I'm safe with you. I'm loved by you.
You are security and
My faith is rising!

That night we danced to Bon Jovi.
You held me.
I held you tight.
You kissed me.
I pulled you in.

It seems like a lifetime of love,
A lifetime of laughter,
and a lifetime of hurt.

Our connection was fierce and eternal,
A fight for the optimum of life lived in front of each other.
A power that could bring life to dead roses …
And oftentimes did.

A love that was too precious to be shared.
A light -- too bright for the world to understand.

Six months later,
You were gone.

Never again will it be like that.

I was in love…
Yes. I was in love … once.

MY HEART IS OPEN

My heart is open;
Come and fill all the holes that are in it.

You make me ready;
I will not be afraid to let you in it.

This place is made for you,
My love is only for you.
Break in with all your power.
Let me see it.
I am ready.

I can see now, you were with me --
Through the pain and through the darkness;
I can feel now.
You have healed me.
Your name is the sweetest.

MY HEART STOPS

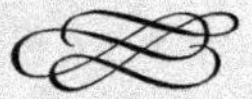

My heart stops.
From all the pain inside.
I reach fast—
Hoping for a line
That can save me from the pit I'm in.
To deliver me from the state I'm in.

Words cannot express how confused I feel inside;
Feelings can't be trusted to reveal the truth inside.
God help me.
God help me.
Teach me to depend on you.

Still --
I'm giving my oil to you.
Still --
I'm giving my all to you.

THE WAY YOU MOVED.

The way that you moved.
The way that you talked.

You looked at me like you wished I was gone.

I never felt safe.

YOUR

Your face
Makes me feel
Exposed and naked.
Transparent in fixation.

Your eyes
Are perfect for gazing
Into you like I would
Into the stars.

Your mind
Challenges the mind
Compelling, sharp, and efficient.
You are unrelenting and cunning.

Betwixt all of these,
That which is yours
Ought not normally perplex
And yet I am lost and pinned into place —
Caught off — and now off balance.

Your heart
Wins mine.
Hands in soil fitting
Like hands on my soul
Pulsate beat and breath is less.
I cannot seem to — catch.

WHAT IS WRONG WITH ME

Feeling locked out of being noticed.

Not engaging me in the back.
Not something I would do.
The second time this has happened --
Is it me?

It's like I'm not interesting.
Thinking I'm just too loud.
Not mysterious enough --
Is it me?

They have never connected like this.
Can't I be selfless?
Can't I be happy for their connection?

I think you are more attractive in this situation
While I feel second on the list
While they forget about me and
Forget to connect

What's my blind spot in this?
Am I overreacting?
Not feeling included, the real question is --
What do I need?

Affirmation. Importance.
Investment. Emotional attachment.
Acknowledgment that something is right with me.

HOW AM I SUPPOSED TO KNOW
IF YOU REALLY CARE

Waiting for the phone to ring
Waiting for the message to ding
But nothing comes through

Holding out and hoping
That one day, you'd turn your head just a little more
Just a little more.

But dreams fade away when you're looking at someone else
I've got to be open to what's next

MIRRORS

Mirror, mirror in my closet.
Who's the horror in the reflection?

"Girl, that's you! Looking FUBU (Fat, Ugly, Black, and
Uncomfortable).
Who do you think you are wearing that ruby red dress
And glass slippers like you've got somewhere to go?
Do you think you're gonna meet a Charming lookin' like that?"

I should smash that mirror.
I would smash if it wasn't the closest thing I had to a friend,
If age wasn't the closest thing I had to the truth.
Shoot, I would believe her over my own mother, know what I
mean?
All mothers think their children are cute.
But the reality is that not all mothers make good people.

THERE IS NO ONE LIKE YOU

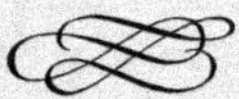

No one that can undo
All the mistakes of the past
You're not intimidated
By the fears and the lies
That keep me from running back to you

But you're beauty lord
That I can't get off my mind
Your ceaseless kindness
Stills my soul every time

Oh, where was I
When you put the stars
In the sky
You know what you're doing

In my life
The battle's all around
But I feel fine

'Cause you know what you're doing
Yes! You know what you're doing.

WHEN YOU LEFT

When you left, the lights were on while the sun shone through
the window.
The condensation from morning's awakening dripping on the
pane.
Sounds of the busy street corner cloud the room.

When you left, I was lying there wondering why you were there
in the first place. Was it a trick? Did you leave because of me?
Were you even real?
A figment of my imagination perhaps driving me to a delusion
of connection
When really you could not truly satisfy.

When you left, I was torn up on the inside.
Despising myself for having let you inside my heart.
I should have been more wise. I should have taken more time.
I should have known that you would die on me and leave me
alone — to fend for myself —
To never find rest.

When you left, I remembered I still loved you more than
anything.
The salt in your hair after the beach that evening,
The color of your eyes and the shape of your face are sung in
my mind — but now fleeting. I'm holding on, but my grip is
slipping.

Remember that time we — gone.
What was our favorite song again? — gone.
Our favorite restaurant? — gone.

When you left, you took them.
You took the memories of our love.
I don't know how to move on.
I don't know how to move.
I don't know —

LONG TIME

It's been such a long time
haven't felt you
in a while

Sometimes I wonder
if you had come —
I'd still be alive.

In those days
There was healing
In those days
They were raising the dead

It's been hard
To live with the silence
But my faith is rising
I know that you'll do it again

Q ...

Q is for query…
not only for the wondering of myself
but also a peculiar curiosity
about the beginning
and about the end.

Q is for quality…
the consideration
of the qualification of our lives
valuable and worth conservation.

Q is for quiet…
that which we cannot be
nor should anyone
sit quietly while our siblings
are taken so quickly
because of ignorance and hate.

Q is for quaking…
yes, that shaking
the awakening we all need
inside ourselves
that we, like you —
have hopes, dreams, and beautiful lives
filled with destiny and promise
so easily swept away by the bullet and pistol.

Q is for quest…
the courageous journey
steadfast we remain
in faith that together
change is well on her way.

JUSTICE FROM THE MOUNTAIN

It is finally springtime here.
Seems to me that people are awakening while winter is passing.
Anticipation is rising, as I feel the slow roll of justice from the
mountain.

We can't see her fully manifested yet,
Which makes us wonder if freedom will ever really come
Or if she is truly of the people, for the people, and by the people.
But my insides creek with assurance that things are coming up
like roses...

Dreams laid dormant are blooming for us.
New positions are opening to us.
Flames shall surely burn in us again.

Open your hands.
Open your heart.
For it is returning — all that was lost.
It is returning.

CONCEIVED IN LOVE

Swallow, gulp.
Enclosed belief.
What are we if not conceived?
What are we if not conceived in love?

But love does seem unfamiliar and fleeting.
The very thing that gave us sentience
is elder magic,
the most powerful of tricks.

One that I've fallen for, and now I am lost.
But I cannot be unless I belong to someone, perhaps because of
love.

Love is the thing we need.
To be free and to belong.

To love then
is to set the bird free from its cage
or to have it captured

for the purpose of nurturing...

One to sacrifice for.
One to adore.
One to hold.
One to behold.

Look up. Filling.
Open your heart.
What are we, if not hopeful in love?
For only in love will we find
the strength to carry,
the faith to try,
and the courage to live fully in love.